To God be the Glory!

Mary Mayer

Where Friends Gather

A Collection of Recipes from the Peppercorn Pantry

MARY MEYER

WESTBOW
PRESS®
A DIVISION OF THOMAS NELSON
& ZONDERVAN

Scriptures taken from the Holy Bible, New International Version®, NIV®. Copyright © 1973, 1978, 1984, 2011 by Biblica, Inc.™ Used by permission of Zondervan. All rights reserved worldwide. www.zondervan.com The "NIV" and "New International Version" are trademarks registered in the United States Patent and Trademark Office by Biblica, Inc.™

WestBow Press books may be ordered through booksellers or by contacting:

WestBow Press
A Division of Thomas Nelson & Zondervan
1663 Liberty Drive
Bloomington, IN 47403
www.westbowpress.com
1 (866) 928-1240

ISBN: 978-1-9736-1674-0 (sc)
ISBN: 978-1-9736-1675-7 (hc)
ISBN: 978-1-9736-1673-3 (e)

Library of Congress Control Number: 2018901248

Printed in the United States of America.

WestBow Press rev. date: 02/01/2018

*To all the people in the body of Christ who have covered
me in prayer, encouragement, and love*

"And let us consider how we may spur one another on toward
love and good deeds, not giving up meeting together, as some
are in the habit of doing, but encouraging one another—
and all the more as you see the Day approaching."
—Hebrews 10:24–25

Contents

Introduction

Rural Iowa is my home and always has been. In my mind, the deep green cornfields topped with golden tassels in early August are one of the most beautiful sights that exist. I have always found joy and satisfaction in witnessing the process of growth, maturity, life, and self-sufficiency, whether it is in farming, gardening, family, or cooking.

I grew up in a family of eleven, and we were of modest means. Mom was particularly gifted in utilizing the food that was available without much waste. I was thrilled when I was finally allowed to cook eggs for all my siblings and quickly memorized how each one preferred his or her eggs.

My joy for cooking and serving others continued through adulthood and ultimately led me to the Peppercorn Pantry, where I discovered my dream. Providing a place for people to gather for fellowship and comforting food has been a delight over the past eleven years. I hope these recipes allow a glimpse into my world of bringing others joy through the art of cooking.

History of the Peppercorn Pantry

The Peppercorn Pantry consists of a gift shop and a tearoom. The building with the gift shop was built in 1858 and once housed a barbershop. The tearoom was built in 1965 and was used as a grocery store for several years. It has been used as a restaurant since 1976.

I purchased the Peppercorn in 2007 and have been running it ever since. In 2009, I purchased the empty lot next door and transformed it into a beautiful patio surrounded by a picturesque garden.

Snacks

In my family, appetizers or snacks just meant the first time you went through the line to eat. These are a few items that we have eaten during football season and some I have used at catering events. I hope you find a few to try at your next gathering.

Beef Crostini

24 slices rye bread

2 tablespoons olive oil

1/2 cup mayonnaise

1/2 cup Parmesan cheese

2 tablespoons chopped chives

2 tablespoons capers, drained

1 teaspoon chopped garlic

1/2 pound deli beef, chopped

1 pint cherry tomatoes

Brush each slice of bread with olive oil and bake on a cookie sheet for 8 to 10 minutes at 350 degrees F. In a bowl, stir together the mayonnaise, Parmesan cheese, chives, capers, garlic, and beef. Spread the mixture on each slice of bread. Top with half of a cherry tomato. Best served warm.

Pinwheels

1/2 pound deli meat, sliced

8 ounces sour cream

8 ounces cream cheese, softened

1/2 cup green onions, chopped

1 cup cheddar cheese, shredded

1/4 teaspoon garlic powder

1/2 cup black olives, sliced

5 large flour tortillas

Combine all the ingredients except the deli meat and spread evenly on each tortilla. Lay deli meat on top of mixture. Roll up tight and press ends together. Refrigerate overnight. Trim ends. Slice to desired thickness and serve.

Spiced Candied Walnuts

peanut oil

1 teaspoon sea salt

1/2 teaspoon black pepper

1/2 teaspoon ground cinnamon

1/2 teaspoon cayenne pepper

4 cups walnut halves

1 cup powdered sugar

Heat at least three inches of oil to 350 degrees F in a fryer or a large stockpot. While the oil is heating up, bring a large pot of water to a boil. Meanwhile, in a medium bowl, combine the sea salt, black pepper, cinnamon, and cayenne pepper. Put the powdered sugar into a separate bowl. Boil the walnuts in the water for approximately 1 minute. Remove the nuts from the water using a sieve and toss them in the powdered sugar until all the sugar has melted. Using a metal slotted spoon, fry the nuts in small batches for 1 minute or until they are medium brown. While the walnuts are still warm, place them in the bowl with the spice mixture and mix well. Cool completely before serving.

Stuffed Mushrooms

16 ounces fresh button mushrooms

8 ounces pork sausage, cooked

1 cup Parmesan cheese

1 cup seasoned bread crumbs

Remove stems from mushrooms, saving caps and about half of the stems. Chop the stems and combine with sausage, cheese, and bread crumbs. Fill the mushroom caps with mixture. Place mushrooms on a cookie sheet and bake at 400 degrees F for 10 to 15 minutes. Serve warm.

Reuben Dip

8 ounces cream cheese

8 ounces sour cream

6 ounces Swiss cheese, shredded

1 pound corned beef, chopped

8 ounces Thousand Island dressing

14 ounces sauerkraut, drained

Combine all the ingredients and heat in a Crock-Pot on high for 1 to 2 hours till hot and bubbly. Serve with rye crisp or crackers.

Guacamole

2 ripe avocados

2 cloves garlic, minced

1 medium red onion

2 Roma tomatoes

2 tablespoons lemon juice

1 teaspoon salt

hot sauce to taste (optional)

1 teaspoon black pepper

Chop or mash the avocados and sprinkle them with lemon juice and salt. Chop or finely dice onions and tomatoes to your liking. Mix all the ingredients together. Serve promptly.

Vegetable Pizza

2 (8-ounce) packages refrigerated crescent rolls

8 ounces cream cheese, softened

1 (4-ounce) package buttermilk dressing mix

4 cups chopped mixed fresh vegetables (broccoli, cauliflower, carrots, tomatoes, celery, onions, peppers, radishes)

8 ounces sour cream

2 cups shredded Colby-Jack cheese

Crust:
Unroll crescent rolls and pat into a 15x10 ungreased baking sheet. Bake at 375 degrees F for 12 minutes or until golden. Cool completely.

Toppings:
In a bowl, stir together cream cheese, sour cream, and dressing mix until smooth. Spread on top of cooled crust. Top with vegetables and sprinkle with cheese. Cut into two-inch squares.

Corn and Black Bean Dip

2 (15.25-ounce) cans corn, drained

2 (15.25-ounce) cans black beans, drained

1 (28-ounce) can diced tomatoes with jalapeños

1 cup green onions, sliced

1/3 cup canola oil

1/3 cup lime juice

1 tablespoon cilantro, chopped

salt and pepper to taste

1 teaspoon cumin

Combine all the ingredients in a large bowl and stir. Cover and refrigerate for 1 to 2 hours before serving.

Dill Pickle Wraps

Always on the table at the Meyer family Christmas

1 pound dried beef

2 (8-ounce) packages cream cheese, softened

1 (32-ounce) jar whole dill pickles

Whip cream cheese in a mixer for 1 to 2 minutes until light and spreadable. Spread cream cheese generously over each slice of dried beef. Roll each pickle in the dried beef and slice into half-inch rounds. Serve immediately or chill and serve later.

Layered Taco Dip

8 ounces cream cheese, softened

8 ounces sour cream

1.25-ounce package taco seasoning

12 ounces cheddar cheese, shredded

1/2 head of lettuce, shredded

2 Roma tomatoes, diced

1 bell pepper, diced

1 large onion, diced

1/2 cup sliced black olives

Mix the cream cheese, sour cream, and taco seasoning together well, and spread on a 9x13 platter. Top with remaining ingredients in the order listed.

Apple Dip

8 ounces cream cheese, softened

1/2 cup sugar

1/2 cup brown sugar

1 teaspoon vanilla

10-ounce bag toffee bits

1/2 cup pecans, chopped

In a medium bowl, cream all ingredients together. Serve with your choice of apples.

Breads

On Mom's day off, she made bread. She would give my twin sister, Martha, and me little pieces of dough to bake in our toy bread pans. I always looked forward to the day Mom made bread.

Banana Muffins

1 cup butter, melted

2 cups sugar

6 bananas, mashed

4 eggs

4 cups flour

1/2 teaspoon salt

2 teaspoons baking soda

2 teaspoons vanilla

Combine dry ingredients in a bowl. In a separate large bowl, add all of the wet ingredients, including mashed bananas. Add dry ingredients to the wet until just blended. Spoon batter into greased muffin tins with 1/3 cup scoop. Bake at 350 degrees F for 18 to 20 minutes. Makes about 2 1/2 dozen.

Bran Muffins

A favorite of the coffee ladies on Thursday mornings

15 ounces bran cereal

1 cup butter, melted

3 cups sugar

4 eggs

4 cups buttermilk

1 teaspoon vanilla

5 teaspoons baking soda

2 teaspoons salt

1 teaspoon cinnamon

6 cups flour

Mix bran cereal with the wet ingredients and let sit for five minutes. In a separate bowl, mix the dry ingredients together. Combine wet and dry ingredients just until blended. Spoon batter into greased muffin tins with 1/3 cup scoop. Bake at 350 degrees F for 18 to 20 minutes. Makes about 2 1/2 dozen.

Glen

My dad, Glen, was a quiet man. So when he spoke, we all listened. Dad grew up on a farm and enjoyed helping make maple syrup with his family every spring. He loved everything about the farm. To this day, Dad's family runs the Green Sugar Bush located near Castalia, Iowa, and makes maple syrup each year. When he was no longer able to farm, he worked at a grain elevator, where he could interact with and help farmers. He loved to drive the gravel roads on the way home from church to look at the fields he had sprayed. He would talk about each field to anyone in the car who would listen. He was always so proud of his children and grandchildren.

Dad served on the *USS Reuben James DE-153* during World War II. He died of cancer in 1994 and is greatly missed.

Maple Muffins

The most requested recipe from patrons of the Peppercorn Pantry

4 cups flour	1 cup butter, melted
4 teaspoons baking powder	1 cup maple syrup
1 teaspoon salt	1/2 cup sour cream
1 cup brown sugar	2 eggs
1 1/2 cups buttermilk	1/2 teaspoon vanilla

Combine the flour, baking powder, salt, and brown sugar. In a separate bowl, mix the wet ingredients together. Add the dry ingredients to the wet and mix until just blended. Spoon batter into greased muffin tins with 1/3 cup scoop. Bake at 350 degrees F for 18 to 20 minutes. Makes 2 dozen.

Morning Glory Muffins

4 cups flour

4 teaspoons baking soda

1 teaspoon salt

4 teaspoons cinnamon

1 1/2 cups sugar

4 cups apples, peeled and grated

1 cup carrots, peeled and grated

1 cup raisins

1 cup shredded coconut

6 eggs

2 cups vegetable oil

4 teaspoons vanilla

Combine the flour, baking soda, salt, and cinnamon in a bowl. In a separate bowl, combine the sugar, apples, carrots, raisins, coconut, eggs, oil, and vanilla. Stir well. Add the dry ingredients to the wet ingredients and mix until just blended. Spoon batter into greased muffin tins with 1/3 cup scoop. Bake at 350 degrees F for 18 to 20 minutes. Makes 2 1/2 to 3 dozen.

Poppy Seed Muffins

3 cups flour

1 1/4 cups sugar

2 teaspoons baking powder

1 1/2 teaspoons salt

1 tablespoon poppy seeds

3/4 cup vegetable oil

1 1/2 cups buttermilk

3 eggs

1/2 teaspoon almond extract

Combine the flour, sugar, baking powder, salt, and poppy seeds. In a separate bowl, combine the wet ingredients. Add the dry ingredients to the wet ingredients and mix until just blended. Spoon batter into greased muffin tins with 1/3 cup scoop. Bake at 350 degrees F for 18 to 20 minutes. Makes 2 dozen.

Pumpkin Muffins

3 1/3 cup flour

2 cups sugar

2 teaspoons baking soda

1 1/2 teaspoons salt

2 teaspoons cinnamon

1 cup vegetable oil

4 eggs

2/3 cup water

2 cups pumpkin

1/2 cup brown sugar

Combine the flour, sugar, baking soda, salt, and cinnamon. In a separate bowl, mix the wet ingredients together. Add the dry ingredients to the wet ingredients and mix until just blended. Spoon batter into greased muffin tins with 1/3 cup scoop. Sprinkle each muffin with 1 teaspoonof brown sugar. Bake at 350 degrees F for 18 to 20 minutes. Makes 2 dozen.

Blueberry Muffins

4 cups flour

2 teaspoons baking powder

1/2 teaspoon baking soda

1 teaspoon salt

4 eggs

1 cup butter, melted

2 cups sugar

2 cups sour cream

2 cups fresh or frozen blueberries(dusted with flour)

Combine the flour, baking powder, baking soda, and salt in a bowl. In a separate bowl, combine the eggs, butter, sugar, and sour cream, and stir well. Mix the two together until just blended. Carefully fold in the blueberries. Spoon batter into greased muffin tins with 1/3 cup scoop. Bake at 350 degrees F for 18 to 20 minutes. Makes 2 dozen.

Zucchini Muffins

3 cups flour	3 eggs
1 teaspoon salt	2 cups sugar
1 teaspoon baking powder	1 tablespoon vanilla
1 teaspoon baking soda	1 cup vegetable oil
1 tablespoon cinnamon	3 cups zucchini, grated

Combine the flour, salt, baking powder, baking soda, and cinnamon in a bowl. In a separate bowl, combine the eggs, sugar, vanilla, vegetable oil, and zucchini, and stir well. Mix the two bowls together just until blended. Spoon batter into greased muffin tins with 1/3 cup scoop. Bake at 350 degrees F for 18 to 20 minutes. Makes 2 dozen.

I have never met anyone who is as selfless, patient, and hardworking as my mother-in-law, Mary. She was raised on the century farm on which we now live and is the fourth generation to be a part of the farm. My son, Zach, is now the sixth generation. She is the definition of an Iowa farm wife. Not only did she keep a clean home, cultivate a garden, cook three meals a day for everyone, and raise two kids, she also spent numerous hours in the tractors doing fieldwork. What I love most about Mary is that she does it all with a smile, humility, and grace. She shows Christ's love to everyone by having a servant's heart.

Overnight Rolls

4 cups water

2 cups sugar

1 cup lard (or margarine)

1 tablespoon salt

2 1/4 teaspoons yeast

4 eggs

12 cups flour

Start making dough at 3:00 p.m. Boil water and sugar in a large saucepan for five minutes. Next add the salt and lard (or margarine). Let mixture cool to lukewarm. After the mixture has cooled, add the yeast and eggs. Mix well. Lastly, add the flour incrementally until it is well-combined and dough has formed. Let rise in a greased bowl until 6:00 p.m. Knead the dough down, form into rolls, and place them in a greased pan or pans at bedtime. Cover the dough and let it rise overnight. Bake in the morning at 350 degrees F for 20 to 30 minutes or until golden brown and the bread sounds hollow. Makes approximately 32 rolls.

Corn Bread

1 cup flour

1 cup cornmeal

2/3 cup sugar

1 teaspoon salt

3 1/2 teaspoons baking powder

1 egg

1 cup milk

1/3 cup vegetable oil

Combine the flour, cornmeal, sugar, salt, and baking powder in a medium bowl. Then add the egg, milk, and oil, and mix until smooth and evenly combined. Pour into a greased 9x9 pan and bake at 400 degrees F for 20 to 25 minutes.

Biscuits

2 cups flour

2 teaspoons sugar

1/2 teaspoon salt

1/2 cup shortening

4 teaspoons baking powder

2/3 cup milk

1/2 teaspoon cream of tartar

Mix the flour, salt, baking powder, cream of tartar, and sugar. Cut in shortening until the mixture resembles coarse crumbs. Add the milk all at once and stir until the dough follows a fork around the bowl. Pat or roll out the dough to a half-inch thick. Cut with a biscuit cutter. Bake at 450 degrees F for 10 to 12 minutes on an ungreased cookie sheet.

Pancakes

2 cups flour

3 teaspoons baking powder

1 teaspoon salt

2 tablespoons sugar

2 eggs

2 cups milk

2 tablespoons oil

Stir dry ingredients together. Make a well in the flour mixture, add the wet ingredients, and beat well. Fry on griddle or pan over medium heat until bubbles form. Flip the pancakes and cook until golden on both sides.

Crepes

1 cup flour	2 large eggs
1/2 teaspoon salt	1 cup whole milk
Pinch of pepper	2 tablespoons butter, melted

In a medium bowl, combine flour, salt, and pepper together. In a separate small bowl, whisk together eggs and milk. Add the wet ingredients to the dry ingredients and mix so there are no lumps, but do not over beat. Add the melted butter to the mixture and stir until just combined. Refrigerate batter for at least an hour. Heat a 10-inch nonstick skillet or crepe pan to medium heat. Pour 1/4 cup of batter onto skillet and tilt the pan to coat evenly. Cook for 50 to 60 seconds. Carefully turn over crepe and cook for additional 10 to 15 seconds. Serve warm.

Classic Cinnamon Coffeecake

A recipe from my sweet daughter-in-law's family

1 beaten egg

1/2 cup sugar

1/2 cup milk

2 tablespoons melted shortening

1 cup flour

1/2 teaspoon salt

2 teaspoons baking powder

Filling:

1/4 cup brown sugar

1 teaspoon cinnamon

1 tablespoon flour

1 tablespoon melted shortening

Combine the egg, sugar, milk, and shortening in a medium bowl. In a separate bowl, sift the flour, salt, and baking powder together. Add the dry ingredients to the wet ingredients and mix well. Pour the batter into a greased 8-inch square pan. Sprinkle with the filling mixture. Bake at 375 degrees F for 20 to 25 minutes.

My son, Caleb, is a special boy in so many ways and has changed the hearts of many over the years. He has some special needs, but we chose to integrate Caleb into public school at Aplington-Parkersburg when he was in sixth grade, and it was the right choice for him. He was able to run track, play football, and even participate in some drama. Caleb loves to work on the farm and help at the Peppercorn.

Several years ago, Caleb started selling cinnamon rolls outside in downtown Aplington on Friday afternoons. 100 percent of the proceeds from his sales are donated to the charity, Feed My Starving Children. It is one of the highlights of his week and we are so proud of his hard work and generosity!

Peppercorn's Cinnamon Rolls

1/4 cup warm water
1/2 tablespoon sugar
1 and 1/2 tablespoons yeast

Combine these three in a bowl and set aside.

2 tablespoons butter	1/3 cup sugar
1/4 cup shortening	1/2 tablespoon salt
1 cup whole milk	3 eggs
3/4 cup warm water	5 1/2–6 cups flour

Filling:
1/2 cup sugar
1 1/2 tablespoons cinnamon
1/4 cup softened butter

Put the butter and shortening in a microwave-safe container and melt on high for 40 seconds. Add the whole milk to the butter mixture and microwave on high for another 40 seconds. Whisk the 3/4 cup of warm water, sugar, salt, and eggs together. Then add the yeast mixture and butter mixture. Whisk again. Stir in 3 cups of flour and continue whisking for 3 to 4 minutes. Add another 2 1/2–3 cups and stir by hand until dough forms. Knead the dough about 100 times. Let rise in a warm place for 1 hour. Roll the dough out to a 24x10-inch rectangle.

Spread 1/4 cup of softened butter on top of the dough. Sprinkle with the sugar and cinnamon. Roll the dough into a long log measuring 24 inches. Cut into 2-inch pieces and set in an 11x15 greased pan.

Bake at 350 degrees F for 24 minutes. Makes 1 dozen. Use frosting recipe at the end of the cake section of this cookbook.

Soups

Chicken Stock

2 whole chickens

3 carrots, peeled

2 cloves garlic, whole

2 large onions

3 stalks celery

1 tablespoon peppercorns

1 tablespoon salt

In an 8-quart stockpot, add the chickens and enough water to cover them. Chop the onions, carrots, and celery in large pieces and add to the pot along with the garlic, salt, and pepper. Bring to a boil and then simmer for 2 hours. Strain. Freeze stock in quart Zip-Lock bags or plastic containers.

Artichoke and Mushroom Soup

1 cup butter

1 (16-ounce) can sliced
mushrooms

1/3 cup dried chopped onion

1 cup flour

8 cups chicken stock

3 (14-ounce) cans artichokes

1 tablespoon onion powder

1/4 teaspoon cayenne pepper

3/4 cup white wine

2 cups half-and-half

Melt butter in a 4-quart stockpot over medium heat. Add flour and stir
to blend. Cook for several minutes, stirring constantly with a whisk or
wooden spoon. Add mushrooms, onions, and chicken stock, stirring
until smooth and slightly thickened. Add artichokes, onion powder,
cayenne pepper, white wine, and half-and-half, stirring until the soup
is heated through. Makes 1 gallon.

Italian Vegetable Soup

1/4 cup olive oil

1 medium onion, chopped

2 garlic cloves, chopped

1 green bell pepper, chopped

1 cup carrots, diced

1 cup celery, diced

3 potatoes, diced

4–5 cups chicken or beef stock

1 (15.5-ounce) can cannellini beans

1 (15.25-ounce) can corn, drained

1 (15-ounce) can tomato sauce

1 (6-ounce) can tomato paste

1 (28-ounce) can diced tomatoes

1 tablespoon dried oregano

1 tablespoon dried basil

1 tablespoon dried thyme

Sauté the onion, garlic, green bell pepper, carrots, and celery in olive oil until soft. Add the potatoes and chicken stock. Simmer until the potatoes are just tender. Add the remaining ingredients, and simmer for 20 minutes over medium heat. Makes 1 gallon.

Chicken Tortilla Soup

1 small whole chicken	1 tablespoon minced garlic
5 cups whole milk	3 cups chicken stock
1 package country gravy mix	32 ounces hash browns, frozen
1/3 cup dried chopped onions	1 pound Velveeta cheese
1 cup celery, sliced thin	1 (8-ounce) can chilies

Bake chicken in a roasting pan at 375 degrees F for 1 hour. Shred chicken. Set aside. Mix 2 cups of milk with the country gravy mix in a bowl and set aside. In a 4-quart stockpot, add 3 cups of milk along with the chicken stock, onions, celery, and garlic. Simmer until the vegetables are soft. Add the hash browns and continue to simmer till they are done (about 15 minutes). Dice the Velveeta cheese, turn off the burner, and add the cheese to the soup. Stir occasionally until the cheese is melted. Turn the burner back on to medium heat. Add the shredded chicken and the milk and gravy mixture to the soup. Heat until warmed through.

Potato Asparagus Soup

1/3 cup dried chopped onions

1/4 cup butter

5 cups chicken stock

7 potatoes, diced

2 pounds asparagus, chopped

1/2 teaspoon pepper

2 tablespoons parsley

1/2 cup instant mashed potatoes (optional)

Place all the ingredients (except the asparagus and instant mashed potatoes) in a heavy stockpot. Simmer until the potatoes are fork tender. Add asparagus and simmer until asparagus is tender. If a thicker soup is desired, add the instant mashed potatoes. Makes 1 gallon.

Almost White Chicken Chili

1/3 cup dried chopped onions

2 (4-ounce) cans green chilies

1 tablespoon cumin

1 tablespoon Southwest
seasoning

1/2 teaspoon cayenne pepper

1 (15.25-ounce) can black beans,
rinsed and drained

6 cups chicken stock

3 (15.8-ounce) cans Great
Northern beans

1 1/2 pounds chicken, shredded

1/4 cup brown sugar

2 cups heavy cream

1/2 cup instant mashed potatoes
(optional)

In a heavy stockpot, add all the ingredients (except the heavy cream) and simmer for 20 minutes. Next add the cream and heat through. If a thicker soup is desired, add 1/2 cup of instant mashed potatoes. Makes 1 gallon.

Wild Rice and Ham Soup

1 cup butter

1/3 cup dried chopped onion

1 cup flour

6 cups chicken stock

1 cup diced ham

4 cups Uncle Ben's Long Grain wild rice, cooked

2 cups carrots, julienned

2 cups half-and-half

1/2 cup white wine

salt and pepper

In a heavy stockpot, melt the butter. Add onion and flour. Stir constantly and cook for 2 to 3 minutes. Add the chicken stock and stir until smooth and slightly thickened. Steam the carrots until just tender in a separate saucepan. Next add the ham, carrots, half-and-half, and wine to the chicken stock mixture. Heat through. Add salt and pepper to taste. Makes 1 gallon.

Wisconsin Cheese Soup

Award-winning soup in 2007

1 cup butter

1 cup flour

1/3 cup dried chopped onions

2 teaspoons dry mustard

1 teaspoons ground black pepper

4 cups whole milk

4 cups chicken stock

12 ounces cream cheese, softened

6 cups broccoli, chopped

3 cups carrots, julienned

16 ounces Velveeta, cubed

4 ounces cheddar cheese, shredded

1 (12-ounce) can beer

Melt butter in a heavy stockpot. Add the flour and cook for several minutes. Stir constantly with a whisk or wooden spoon. Next, add the onions, mustard, and pepper. Add cream cheese and stir until melted. Add the milk and chicken stock, stirring until smooth and hot. Turn the burner off and add Velveeta cheese. Stir constantly until it has melted. Keep the pot on low heat. In a separate pot, steam broccoli and carrots until tender. Add the vegetables and beer to the soup and heat through. Makes 1 gallon.

Cheesy Vegetable Soup

7 cups chicken stock

2 1/2 cups carrots, chopped

2 1/2 cups celery, chopped

6 potatoes, chopped

1/3 cup dried chopped onions

2 tablespoons dried parsley

1 pound Velveeta cheese, cubed

1 cup half-and-half

salt and pepper

1/2 cup instant mashed potatoes (optional)

Simmer all the vegetables in chicken stock until tender. Turn off the burner and add the Velveeta. Let soup sit for 10 minutes. Then stir to make sure the cheese is melted. Turn burner back on to medium heat and add the half-and-half and instant potatoes if desired. Season with salt and pepper to taste. Makes 1 gallon.

Vegetable Chili

1 pound ground beef

2 bell peppers, chopped

1 large onion, chopped

1 tablespoon garlic, minced

1 (48-ounce) can diced tomatoes

1 (40-ounce) can chili beans

1 teaspoon oregano, dried

3 tablespoons chili powder

2 tablespoons Worcestershire sauce

1 (4-ounce) can sliced mushrooms

1 (2.25-ounce) can sliced black olives

1/2 cup green olives, sliced

Brown ground beef over medium-high heat along with peppers, onions, and garlic in a stockpot. Add the remaining ingredients and simmer for 20 to 30 minutes over medium heat. Makes 1 gallon.

Tomato Bisque

The most popular soup at the Peppercorn Pantry

4 cups chicken stock

4 (28-ounce) cans crushed
tomatoes

1/4 cup butter

1/3 cup dried chopped onions

1/2 teaspoon baking soda

1/2 cup sugar

1 (6-ounce) can tomato paste

2 cups heavy cream

2 tablespoons dried parsley

Combine all the ingredients in a stockpot except the tomato paste and cream. Simmer for 20 minutes. Then add tomato paste and cream, mixing until evenly heated. Add dried parsley if desired. Makes 1 gallon.

Iowa Corn Chowder

5 potatoes, cubed

5 slices bacon

1 (15.25 ounce) can whole kernel corn

2 (14.75-ounce) cans creamed corn

6 cups chicken stock

2 cups half-and-half

1 teaspoon salt

1/2 teaspoon pepper

1/2 cup butter

1/3 cup dried onion

Fry bacon, crumble, and set aside. In heavy stockpot, simmer potatoes and onions in chicken stock until tender. Add corn, half-and-half, salt, pepper, and butter, and simmer for 20 minutes. Makes 1 gallon.

Chicken Noodle Soup

10 cups chicken stock

3 cups carrots, chopped

3 cups celery, chopped

1 (24-ounce) package frozen egg noodles

1/3 cup dried chopped onions

4 cups diced chicken, cooked

2 tablespoons parsley, dried

salt and pepper

In a heavy stockpot, simmer the stock, carrots, celery, and onions until tender. Add chicken and noodles. Bring to a boil until the noodles are cooked. Add parsley. Season with salt and pepper to taste. Makes 1 gallon.

Sausage and Potato Soup

1 pound sausage

1 large onion, chopped

2 tablespoons garlic, minced

4 slices bacon, chopped

10 cups chicken stock

6 potatoes, chopped

6 ounces fresh kale, chopped

1 cup heavy cream

Salt and pepper

In a heavy stockpot, brown the sausage, onion, garlic, and bacon. Add chicken stock, potatoes, and kale. Simmer until potatoes are tender. Add cream. Season to taste. Makes 1 gallon.

Loaded Potato Soup

1 cup butter

1 cup flour

6 cups whole milk

1 cup sour cream

7 baked potatoes, diced

1/3 cup dried chopped onions

1 teaspoon salt

1/2 teaspoon pepper

6 slices bacon, fried

1 cup shredded cheddar cheese

In a heavy stockpot, melt the butter. Then add the flour and cook for several minutes, stirring constantly with a whisk or wooden spoon. Add milk, sour cream, salt, and pepper. Stir until smooth. Next add potatoes, onions, bacon, and cheese. Heat through. Makes 1 gallon.

Sweet Potato Corn Chowder

6 slices bacon, chopped

1/2 cup flour

5 cups chicken stock

1/3 cup dried chopped onion

1 tablespoon garlic, minced

2 cups celery, chopped

1 (15.25-ounce) can sweet corn

5 cups sweet potatoes, peeled and diced

1 cup heavy cream

In a heavy stockpot, brown the bacon over medium-high heat until almost crisp. Remove bacon and set aside. Add the flour and cook for several minutes, stirring constantly with a whisk or wooden spoon. Add chicken stock and the remaining ingredients. Simmer until the sweet potatoes are tender. Makes 1 gallon.

Chicken Pot Pie Soup

5–6 cups chicken stock

2 cups celery, chopped

2 cups carrots, chopped

4 potatoes, chopped

1/3 cup dried chopped onion

2 teaspoons salt

1 teaspoon pepper

1/2 cup butter

2 cups frozen peas

4 cups chicken, shredded

1/2 cup instant mashed potatoes (optional)

Combine all the ingredients except the peas and chicken. Simmer until the vegetables are tender. Add the peas and chicken, and heat through. If the soup is not thick enough, add 1/2 cup instant mashed potatoes. Pour the soup in medium-sized soup bowls and top with your favorite piecrust. Bake at 450 degrees F for 10 to 15 minutes.

Split Pea Soup

1/3 cup dried chopped onion

2 cups carrots, diced

1 teaspoon minced garlic

2 potatoes, diced

2 cups dried split peas

2 teaspoons salt

8 cups chicken stock

1 teaspoon pepper

Combine all the ingredients in a heavy stockpot and simmer until the peas are cooked (about 40 to 60 minutes). Stir frequently so the solids do not burn on the bottom of the pot. Makes 1 gallon.

White Bean Soup

4 strips of bacon, cooked

2 (15-ounce) cans cannellini beans

1/3 cup dried chopped onion

1 cup celery, diced

1 cup carrots, diced

1 tablespoon garlic, chopped

1 bay leaf

6 cups chicken stock

salt and pepper to taste

1/4 teaspoon red pepper flakes

1/4 cup fresh basil, chiffonade (optional)

1/4 cup extra virgin olive oil

In a large stockpot, simmer all ingredients together for 20 to 30 minutes over medium heat until vegetables are tender. Remove from heat and let cool for 30 minutes. Purée the soup in batches in a food processor. Return to the pot and add olive oil. Bring soup to a simmer over medium heat. Add fresh basil (if desired) and serve. Makes 1 gallon.

My dream came to life when I married a farmer (my high school sweetheart, nonetheless). Russ was more mature than any boy I had ever met and made me laugh. Throughout the years, he has worked tirelessly out of devotion to the farm and his family. I look forward to growing old together with him.

When I purchased the Peppercorn Pantry, we went grocery shopping together on a weekly basis. We would grab two carts. I had the Peppercorn's cart and he had the cart for home. Naturally we had a friendly competition to see who could finish his or her shopping first. During these shopping trips, Russ set out to create his ideal chili recipe. Each week he experimented with different beans and ingredients until he came up with this combination.

The Husband's Chili

2 pounds ground beef

1 large onion, chopped

1 teaspoon pepper

1 teaspoon salt

1 teaspoon garlic powder

1 tablespoon chili powder

1 (27-ounce) can Bush's mild chili beans

1 (28-ounce) can Bush's honey baked beans

1 (28-ounce) can petite diced tomatoes

tomato juice

In a large stockpot, brown beef with the onions and seasonings. Add the beans and tomatoes. Fill pot with tomato juice and bring to a simmer for 20 minutes before serving.

Minestrone

1/4 pound Mafalda pasta

1 pound mild pork sausage

8 cups chicken broth

2 cups carrots, diced

1/3 cup dried chopped onions

2 cups finely shredded cabbage

2 potatoes, finely diced

2 tablespoons tomato paste

1 (28-ounce) can diced tomatoes

2 (28-ounce) cans cannellini beans

1 tablespoon garlic, minced

2 teaspoons dried oregano

1 teaspoon salt

1 teaspoon black pepper

1 1/2 teaspoons dried basil

3 tablespoons dried parsley

Bring a small pot of salted water to a boil and cook the Mafalda until slightly underdone. Drain and set aside. In a large stockpot, brown sausage until done. Then add the chicken broth, carrots, potatoes, onions, cabbage, garlic, oregano, salt, pepper, and basil. Simmer until vegetables are tender. Add tomatoes and beans. Simmer for another 10 minutes. Then add the tomato paste. Add the cooked Mafalda and parsley. Makes 1 gallon.

Salads

Poppy Seed Chicken Salad

Served daily at the tearoom

12 roasted chicken breasts

1 cup mayonnaise

1 cup sour cream

1/2 cup honey

1 tablespoon poppy seeds

2 cups grapes, halved

1 cup celery, sliced

salt and pepper

Shred chicken. In a large bowl, combine all the ingredients and mix well. Salt and pepper to taste.

Chicken and Wild Rice Salad

6 roasted chicken breasts

4 cups cooked wild rice

1 cup mayonnaise

1/2 cup milk

2 tablespoons lemon juice

1 teaspoon dried tarragon

1/3 cup dried chopped onion

1 (8-ounce) can water chestnuts

1 teaspoon salt

1/2 teaspoon pepper

1 cup grapes, halved

1 cup salted cashews

Shred chicken. Drain the water chestnuts. In a large bowl, combine all the ingredients and mix well. Chill and serve.

Julia. I love that name. She is my only daughter, and I am okay with that. She was a tough little girl who grew up surrounded by boys and her interest in dolls lasted about a month. She has always loved to read and write, and she is such a good helper.

I admire all she has accomplished and love to spend time with her now that she is grown. It's a bonus that she has also given me three adorable grandchildren!

Chunky Fruited Chicken Salad

A favorite of my daughter, Julia

6 roasted chicken breasts

1 (20-ounce) can pineapple chunks, drained

1 cup grapes, halved

1 cup celery, diced

1/3 cup dried chopped onions

2 apples, chopped

1 cup mayonnaise

1 teaspoon curry powder

salt and pepper

Shred chicken. Combine all the ingredients in a large bowl. Mix well. Salt and pepper to taste. Chill and serve.

Cashew Chicken Salad

6 roasted chicken breasts

1 cup celery, sliced

1 green bell pepper, chopped

1 cup mayonnaise

1/2 cup whole milk

1 cup sour cream

1/3 cup dried chopped onion

2 tablespoons dried parsley

2 teaspoons lemon juice

2 teaspoons cider vinegar

1 tablespoon garlic, minced

1/2 teaspoon pepper

3/4 cup cashews, halves and pieces

Shred chicken. Make the sauce by combining the mayonnaise, milk, sour cream, onion, parsley, lemon juice, vinegar, garlic, and pepper. Mix chicken, vegetables, cashews, and sauce together. Chill and serve.

Southwestern Chicken Salad

My personal favorite salad

6 roasted chicken breasts

1 (15.5-ounce) can red beans, drained

1 green bell pepper, chopped

1/3 cup dried chopped onion

1 cup sliced black olives

1 cup shredded cheddar cheese

1 cup sour cream

1/2 cup mayonnaise

1 tablespoon cumin

1 tablespoon Southwest seasoning

1 (7-ounce) can green chilies

Shred chicken. In a large bowl, combine all ingredients and mix well. Chill and serve.

This salad can be served on lettuce, with chips, or rolled in tortillas.

Pecan Chicken Salad

6 roasted chicken breasts

2 cups grapes, halved

2 tablespoons whole grain mustard

1/3 cup dried chopped onions

5 slices bacon

1 cup sour cream

1 cup mayonnaise

1 teaspoon salt

1/2 teaspoon pepper

1 cup chopped pecans

Shred chicken. Fry bacon over medium-high heat just until crisp. Let bacon cool and crumble into pieces. In a large bowl, combine all the ingredients and mix well. Chill and serve.

Asian Chicken Salad

6 roasted chicken breasts

4 cups shredded cabbage

1/2 cup salted cashews

8 ounces Asian ginger dressing

1/3 cup sesame seeds

1 cup dried pineapple

3 green onions, sliced

1 red bell pepper, sliced thin

Shred chicken. Mix all ingredients together with the dressing. Either chill or serve at room temperature.

Crab Louie

Served daily at the Peppercorn

1/2 cup sour cream

1/2 cup mayonnaise

1/4 cup chili sauce

2 teaspoons lemon juice

1 pound imitation crab

1/2 teaspoon salt

1/2 teaspoon pepper

2 tablespoons dried chopped onion

1/2 teaspoon dill weed

Shred crab. In a medium bowl, mix together all the ingredients. Chill and serve. May be garnished with hard-boiled eggs, tomatoes, and/or cucumbers.

Tuna with a Twist

4(12-ounce) cans tuna

1 cup chopped cucumbers

1 (2.25-ounce) can sliced black olives

1/2 cup chopped red bell pepper

1/3 cup dried chopped onions

1 cup celery, sliced

1 cup mayonnaise

1 cup sour cream

1 tablespoon Dijon mustard

1 teaspoon lemon pepper

1 teaspoon dill weed

1 teaspoon minced garlic

Drain tuna. Mix together all the ingredients except the tuna. Gently stir in the tuna, trying to keep it chunky. Chill and serve.

Broccoli Grape Salad

Loaded with extra toppings

1 cup mayonnaise

1 teaspoon vinegar

1/3 cup sugar

4 cups chopped broccoli

2 cups grapes, halved

1/2 cup green onions, sliced

1 cup chopped celery

2/3 cup sliced almonds

1/2 cup sunflower seeds

1/2 cup pumpkin seeds

1/2 cup raisins

1/2 cup dried cranberries

6 slices bacon, fried

Mix together the mayonnaise, vinegar, and sugar in a large bowl and let it sit for 5 to 10 minutes until sugar has dissolved. Combine with the rest of the ingredients and serve within 30 minutes to ensure the vegetables remain crisp.

Mary's Potato Salad

7 potatoes

7 eggs

1/4 cup dried chopped onions

1/2 cup ranch dressing

1 cup mayonnaise

1/2 cup sour cream

2 tablespoons pickle relish

1 tablespoon mustard

1 teaspoon salt

1/2 teaspoon black pepper

Boil the potatoes until tender and set aside to cool. Boil the eggs for 10 minutes and take them out of the pot. Set aside to cool. When the eggs and potatoes are cool enough, peel them. Put both in the fridge to chill. Either shred the potatoes and eggs in a food processor using a large grating blade or dice by hand. Add the remaining ingredients and mix well. Chill and serve.

Vegetables

Macaroni & Corn

1 (15.25-ounce) can whole kernel corn, undrained

1 (14.75-ounce) can cream style corn

1 cup uncooked macaroni

1/2 cup melted butter

salt and pepper to taste

1 cup cheddar cheese, shredded

Combine both cans of corn with the macaroni and place in an 8x8 greased baking dish. Top with salt, pepper, butter, and cheese. Bake at 350 degrees F for 1 hour.

Mary's Cheesy Potatoes

A catering favorite

8 potatoes, boiled and unpeeled

1 (10.5-ounce) can condensed cream of chicken soup

10.5 ounces whole milk

1/2 cup sour cream

2 cups shredded cheddar cheese

salt, pepper, and garlic powder

1/2 cup butter

Dice the potatoes after they have cooled. Place half of the potatoes in a greased 9x13 baking dish. Sprinkle with salt, pepper, garlic powder, and half of the cheese. Cut butter into small pieces and sprinkle over cheese. Repeat with another layer of potatoes, followed by more salt, pepper, garlic powder, remaining cheese, and the other half of the butter. Mix the soup and the soup can full of milk along with the sour cream together until smooth. Pour the mixture over potatoes. Bake in a covered dish for 1 hour at 350 degrees F.

Scalloped Corn

4 cups canned whole kernel corn   1 egg

1 cup cracker crumbs   1 1/2 cups whole milk

1 teaspoon salt   1/2 teaspoon pepper

Combine all the ingredients and place into a 1 1/2-quart greased casserole dish. Bake at 325 degrees F for 30 minutes.

Creamy Corn

20-ounce bag corn, frozen or fresh

1 cup butter, softened

8 ounces cream cheese

3 tablespoons sugar

salt and pepper

Soften cream cheese in the microwave. Mix all the ingredients together. Salt and pepper to taste. Pour into a small greased casserole dish. Bake at 350 degrees F for 1 hour.

Sweet Potato Bake

3 large sweet potatoes

1 cup sugar

1 teaspoon salt

1/2 teaspoon pepper

2 eggs, beaten

1/2 cup melted butter

1/2 cup whole milk

Topping:

1 cup brown sugar

1 cup chopped pecans

1/3 cup flour

1/4 cup melted butter

Boil the sweet potatoes until tender. Peel and mash. In a mixing bowl, combine sweet potatoes with the sugar, salt, pepper, eggs, butter, and milk. Place in a greased 9x13 baking dish. Next combine the topping ingredients and sprinkle over the sweet potato mixture. Bake at 350 degrees F for 45 minutes.

Main Dishes

Peppercorn Quiche

9 1/2-inch unbaked pie shell

4 cups chopped broccoli,

8 ounces ham, chopped

4 slices bacon, chopped

5 ounces shredded cheddar cheese

7 ounces shredded Swiss cheese

8 eggs

3/4 cup half-and-half

Salt and pepper

nutmeg

Steam the broccoli until crisp-tender. Fry bacon. Place the broccoli in the unbaked pie shell. Sprinkle with salt and pepper. Then layer the ham, bacon, cheddar, and Swiss. In a medium bowl, whisk together the eggs and half-and-half. Sprinkle with nutmeg. Bake at 350 degrees F for 35 minutes. Cover and bake for an additional 35 minutes. Let dish cool for 10 minutes before serving.

Spinach Pie

9 1/2-inch unbaked pie shell

12 ounces fresh spinach, chopped

4 ounces cream cheese, softened

8 ounces shredded cheddar cheese

1/3 cup dried chopped onion

1–2 tomatoes, depending on size

2 tablespoons dried parsley

1/2 teaspoon salt

1/2 teaspoon pepper

7 eggs

2/3 cup Parmesan cheese

In a medium bowl, combine spinach and cream cheese. Stir until the cream cheese is evenly distributed throughout the spinach. Add the cheddar cheese, parsley, salt, pepper, eggs, and onion. Blend well. Pour into unbaked pie shell.

Sprinkle half of the Parmesan cheese on top of the egg mixture. Slice tomatoes very thin and cover pie. Then sprinkle with the other half of the Parmesan cheese. Bake at 350 degrees F for 35 minutes. Cover and bake an additional 35 minutes. Let dish cool for 10 minutes before serving.

Quiche Lorraine

9 1/2-inch unbaked pie shell

6 slices bacon, chopped

1/3 cup dried chopped onion

16 ounces shredded Swiss cheese, divided

9 eggs

1 cup half-and-half

Salt and pepper

nutmeg

Fry bacon. Layer 8 ounces of shredded Swiss cheese in the unbaked pie shell. Top with salt, pepper, onions, and bacon. Sprinkle remaining 8 ounces of shredded Swiss on top of the bacon. Whisk eggs and half-and- half in a medium bowl and pour into crust. Sprinkle with nutmeg. Bake at 350 degrees F for 35 minutes. Cover and bake for another 35 minutes. Let dish cool for 10 minutes before serving.

Asparagus Quiche

9 1/2-inch unbaked pie shell

6 slices bacon, chopped

1/3 cup dried chopped onions

10 ounces shredded Swiss cheese

8 ounces asparagus, frozen or fresh

9 eggs

1 cup half-and-half

1/2 teaspoon salt

1/2 teaspoon pepper

Fry bacon. In a medium bowl, mix all ingredients together. Pour into pie shell. Sprinkle the top with coarse ground black pepper. Bake at 350 degrees F for 35 minutes. Cover and bake for another 35 minutes. Let dish cool for 10 minutes before serving.

Steak and Mushrooms

1/2 cup butter

1 cup fresh mushroom, sliced

1/2 cup onions, sliced

1 tablespoon minced garlic

1 teaspoon lemon juice

1 teaspoon Worcestershire sauce

pinch of salt and pepper

1 tablespoon fresh parsley

1 pound beef tenderloin

In a large skillet, melt 4 tablespoons of butter over medium heat. Add the mushrooms, onions, garlic, lemon juice, Worcestershire sauce, salt, and pepper. Sauté until mushrooms are tender. In another large skillet, melt the other 4 tablespoons of butter. Cook steak over medium-high heat for 3 minutes on each side. Pour mushroom mixture over the steak and serve.

Porcupine Meatballs

My mother's recipe

1 1/2 pounds hamburger

1/2 cup rice, uncooked

1 teaspoon salt

1 teaspoon pepper

1 tablespoon onion powder

1 can (10.75-ounce) tomato soup

1 cup water

Mix together everything except soup and water. Form into balls approximately 1 inch in diameter. Place meatballs in a Dutch oven. Combine tomato soup and water, and pour over meatballs. Bake for 90 minutes at 350 degrees F.

Chicken Florentine Lasagna

1/2 cup butter

1 medium onion, chopped

2 teaspoons minced garlic

1/2 cup flour

1 1/2 cups whole milk

4 1/2 cups shredded mozzarella cheese

1 1/2 cup Parmesan cheese

12 ounces fresh spinach, chopped

16 ounces lasagna noodles, cooked

1 tablespoon dried basil

1 teaspoon dried oregano

1 teaspoon black pepper

15 ounces ricotta cheese

1 tablespoon dried parsley

3 cups chicken, shredded

Sauté the onion and garlic in the butter until tender. Whisk in the flour and cook for several minutes. Stir constantly with whisk or wooden spoon. Slowly add milk until the mixture is smooth. Bring to a boil and stir until thickened, about 5 to 10 minutes. To this mixture, add 2 cups mozzarella cheese and 1/2 cup Parmesan cheese.

Place chopped spinach in a medium bowl. Pour half of the cheese mixture into this bowl and add the basil, oregano, pepper, ricotta cheese, parsley, 2 more cups of mozzarella, and 1/2 cup Parmesan cheese.

Grease a 9x13 pan. Layer 1/3 of the noodles, 1/2 of the spinach mixture, 1/2 of the shredded chicken, and 1/3 of the cheese sauce. Repeat. Top with a third layer of noodles, the remaining cheese sauce, remaining mozzarella, and Parmesan. Bake at 350 degrees F for 45 minutes or until bubbly. Let it cool for 10 to 15 minutes before serving.

Cordon Bleu Casserole

6 cups cooked white rice

3 cups corned beef, diced

5 cups cooked chicken, diced

1 cup shredded Swiss cheese

1/3 cup dried chopped onion

1 cup butter

1 cup flour

4 cups whole milk

1 teaspoon dill weed

1 teaspoon dry mustard

1/4 teaspoon nutmeg

Topping

1 cup bread crumbs

2 tablespoons melted butter

1/2 teaspoon dill weed

1/2 cup shredded Swiss cheese

Place rice on the bottom of a greased 10x15 pan. Spread the beef, chicken, cheese, and onions evenly over the rice. Melt butter in heavy 4-quart pan. Whisk in flour. Cook for 2 minutes and stir constantly with a whisk or wooden spoon. Then slowly add the milk and whisk until smooth and thick. Add dill weed, dry mustard, and nutmeg to the pan. Pour the sauce over chicken and beef layers. Mix the topping ingredients and spread over the sauce. Bake at 350 degrees F for 45 to 60 minutes.

Country Chicken Bake

1/2 loaf sandwich bread, cubed

3 roasted chicken breasts

2 cups celery, sliced thin

2 tablespoons dried chopped onions

1 cup Miracle Whip

1 (8-ounce) can sliced water chestnuts

1/2 red bell pepper, chopped

3 eggs

2 cups whole milk

1 (10.5-ounce) can cream of chicken soup

1/2 cup mayonnaise

1 cup shredded cheddar cheese

1 teaspoon salt, divided

1 teaspoon pepper, divided

1 tablespoon rubbed sage, divided

Grease a 9x13 pan. Place half of the bread on the bottom of the pan. Sprinkle generously with 1/2 teaspoon salt, 1/2 teaspoon pepper, and 1/2 tablespoon sage. In a medium bowl, combine chicken, celery, onions, Miracle Whip, water chestnuts, and red bell pepper. Spread over the bread. Cover with the other half of the bread. Sprinkle again with remaining salt, pepper, and sage.

In the same bowl, whisk together the eggs and milk. Pour over all the layers. At this point, either refrigerate this overnight or continue. Cover and bake at 325 degrees F for 75 minutes. In a small bowl, mix together cream of chicken soup and mayonnaise. Take casserole out of the oven and pour the soup mixture over it. Top with shredded cheddar cheese. Cover again and continue baking for an additional 15 minutes. Let it cool for 10 to 15 minutes before serving.

Poppy Seed Chicken

8 chicken breasts

3 tablespoons oil

1 (10.5-ounce) can cream of
chicken soup

16 ounces sour cream

1/2 cup melted butter

2 rolls butter cracker crumbs

3 tablespoons poppy seeds

Grease a 9x10 pan. In a frying pan, sauté the chicken breasts in oil for
2 minutes on each side over medium heat. Lay them in a single layer
in the baking dish. In a medium bowl, mix cream of chicken soup and
sour cream until smooth. Spread over chicken. In a small bowl, mix
together the cracker crumbs, butter, and poppy seeds. Spread this over
the cream layer. Cover and bake at 350 degrees F for 1 hour. Serve over
rice, pasta, or alone.

Herbed Stuffed Chicken

8 chicken breasts

8 ounces cream cheese, softened

1 teaspoon dried oregano

1 teaspoon dried basil

1 teaspoon dried dill weed

1 teaspoon garlic powder

1 teaspoon dried tarragon

1 teaspoon pepper

2 cups bread crumbs

4 tablespoons melted butter

2 tablespoons dried parsley

Pound chicken flat and set aside. In a medium bowl or mixer, thoroughly blend the cream cheese, oregano, basil, dill, garlic powder, tarragon, and pepper. Equally divide the cream cheese mixture and place on top of the chicken breasts. Roll the breast up and place them seam down in a greased pan. Combine bread crumbs, butter, and parsley. Sprinkle on top of the chicken. Bake in a covered dish at 350 degrees F for 1 hour.

Baby Bella Chicken

8 chicken breasts

3 tablespoons bacon grease or butter

16 ounces Bella mushrooms, fresh

1/2 cup onions, chopped

1/4 cup flour

1 cup whole milk

1 cup chicken stock

1/3 cup white wine

1 teaspoon thyme, dried

1 teaspoon basil, dried

5 Roma tomatoes, chopped and seeded

In a frying pan, sauté chicken over medium heat for 2 minutes on each side using either bacon grease or butter. Place the chicken in a greased 9x15 baking dish. In the same skillet, add onions and sliced mushrooms, and sauté over medium heat until soft. Add flour and cook for several minutes, stirring constantly with whisk or wooden spoon. Slowly add the milk and then the stock. Simmer until the sauce thickens. Add the wine and spices. Pour the sauce over the chicken. Top with tomatoes. In a covered dish, bake at 350 degrees F for 1 hour.

Chicken Florentine

8 chicken breasts

3 tablespoons oil

1 cup butter

1 cup flour

3 cups whole milk

1 teaspoon garlic, minced

1/4 teaspoon cayenne pepper

1 teaspoon Worcestershire sauce

10 ounces fresh spinach

1 cup shredded cheddar cheese

1 cup bread crumbs

dried parsley

1/4 cup melted butter

Sauté chicken in a skillet in oil over medium heat for 2 minutes on each side. Set aside on a plate. In the same skillet, add butter until melted, and then add flour. Cook for several minutes and stir constantly with a whisk or wooden spoon. Slowly add the milk and cook until thickened. Add the garlic, cayenne pepper, and Worcestershire sauce. Roughly chop the spinach and place in a bowl. Pour half of the milk mixture over the spinach. Add the cheese to the remaining milk mixture. In a greased 9x13 baking dish, layer the spinach mixture, chicken, and cheese sauce. Top with bread crumbs. Sprinkle parsley and melted butter on top of the bread crumbs. In a covered dish, bake at 350 degrees F for 1 hour.

Chicken Parisian

8 chicken breasts

3 tablespoons oil

1 (10.5-ounce) can cream of mushroom soup

2 (4-ounce) cans of sliced mushrooms

1 cup sour cream

1/2 cup white wine

3/4 cup Parmesan cheese

dried parsley (optional)

Sauté chicken in a skillet with oil on medium heat for 2 minutes on each side. Place the chicken in a greased 9x13 baking dish. Combine soup, mushrooms, sour cream, and wine in a medium mixing bowl. Pour over the chicken and top with Parmesan cheese. You may add parsley for color. In a covered dish, bake at 350 degrees F for 1 hour.

Creamy Apricot Chicken

8 chicken breasts

4 tablespoons oil

4 tablespoons butter

1/3 cup flour

1 chicken bouillon cube
(optional)

Salt and pepper to taste

2 cups whole milk

8–16 dried apricots

1/3 cup dried chopped onions

Sauté chicken in a skillet in oil over medium heat for 2 minutes on each side. Place in a greased 9x13 baking dish. Add butter to the skillet. Add flour and cook several minutes, stirring constantly with a whisk or wooden spoon. At this time, add 1 chicken bouillon cube (if desired). Alternatively, add salt to taste. Slowly add the milk and simmer until thick, stirring constantly. On each chicken breast, place 1 to 2 apricots. Sprinkle with onions. Pour white sauce over chicken. In a covered dish, bake at 350 degrees F for 1 hour.

Orange Almond Chicken

8 chicken breasts

3 tablespoons oil

1 (15-ounce) can mandarin oranges

1/3 cup sliced almonds

1 tablespoon Dijon mustard

2 tablespoons orange marmalade

dash cayenne pepper

2 chicken bouillon cubes

2 cups heavy cream

Sauté chicken in skillet with oil over medium heat for 2 minutes on each side. Place in a greased 9x13 baking dish. Drain the liquid off the oranges into the skillet, deglazing the pan. Sprinkle the oranges on the chicken followed by the sliced almonds. In the skillet, add mustard, marmalade, cayenne pepper, and bouillon cubes. Simmer until all is dissolved. Add cream and simmer until slightly thickened, stirring occasionally. Pour sauce over chicken. In a covered dish, bake at 350 degrees F for 1 hour.

Spinach Stuffed Chicken with Raspberry Sauce

8 chicken breasts	2 eggs
10 ounces fresh spinach, chopped	4 slices bacon, halved
1 cup shredded Swiss cheese	fresh ground black pepper
1 cup Parmesan cheese	1/2 cup raspberry vinaigrette

Pound each chicken breast until thin. Set aside. In a medium bowl, mix together the spinach, Swiss and Parmesan cheeses, and eggs. Divide equally into 8 parts. Lay chicken breast silver skin down. Place cheese-spinach mixture on each breast and roll. Place in a greased 9x13 baking dish with the seam down. Place the halved bacon pieces on top of the rolled chicken. Sprinkle with fresh ground pepper. In a covered dish, bake at 350 degrees F for 1 hour. Before serving, top each chicken breast with 1 tablespoon raspberry vinaigrette.

Parmesan Crusted Cod

8 (6-ounce) cod fillets

1 1/2 cups heavy cream

2 cups bread crumbs

1 cup Parmesan cheese

4 tablespoons butter, melted

1 teaspoon dry mustard

1 teaspoon salt

1 teaspoon garlic powder

2 teaspoons dried parsley

Place cod in a greased 9x13 baking dish. Pour cream over the cod. In a medium bowl, combine the rest of the ingredients and mix well. Place a generous handful of crumb mixture on each cod fillet. Bake in an uncovered dish at 350 degrees F for 30 to 40 minutes.

Salmon with Creamy Lemon Dill Sauce

8 (6-ounce) salmon fillets

1/2 cup lemon juice

1 cup white wine

Lemon pepper and dill weed

4 tablespoons butter

1/4 cup dried chopped onion

1 chicken bouillon cube

1 tablespoon Dijon mustard

2 tablespoons lemon juice

4 tablespoons white wine

1 cup heavy cream

Place fillets in a greased 9x13 baking dish. Pour 1/2 cup of lemon juice and 1 cup of wine over fillets. Sprinkle lightly with lemon pepper and dill. In a covered dish, bake at 350 degrees F for 30 minutes.

While salmon is in the oven, melt butter in a skillet over medium heat. Stir in the onion, bouillon, mustard, 2 tablespoons lemon juice, 4 tablespoons wine, and a dash of dill weed. Cook until slightly bubbly. Add cream and simmer, stirring occasionally, until reduced almost by half. Serve over salmon.

Lemon Peppered Cod

8 (6-ounce) cod fillets

1/2 cup lemon juice

1 cup white wine

lemon pepper

dill weed

Place fillets in a greased baking dish. Pour lemon juice and wine over fillets. Sprinkle lightly with both lemon pepper and dill weed. Bake in a covered dish at 350 degrees F for 30 to 45 minutes.

As a little girl, nothing brought me more joy than going to Grandma Evelyn's house. Grandpa and Grandma's house was as perfect as a postcard. There was a red building, a white house, livestock, and beautiful flowers. The week I spent at their house with my sister Martha was a wonderful experience. Grandma taught us to iron, cook, bake, wash dishes, set the table, and do chores. My favorite thing Grandma taught us was how to deadhead flowers. It was then that I knew I was hooked on gardening.

Throughout the following years, Grandma Evelyn continued to inspire me with her kindness, etiquette, and faith. I only hope that my grandchildren long to spend time with me in the same way I did with Grandma Hawkins.

Evelyn's Ham Balls

2 1/2 pounds ground ham

2 pounds ground pork

1 pound ground beef

3 eggs

2 cups whole milk

2 sleeves graham crackers, crushed

2 (10.75-ounce) cans tomato soup

2 1/2 cups brown sugar

3/4 cup white vinegar

2 teaspoons dry mustard

Mix the ham, pork, beef, eggs, milk, and graham crackers together just until blended. Using a 1/3 cup ice cream scoop, form balls and place them into two greased 9x13 baking dishes. Combine the tomato soup, brown sugar, vinegar, and dry mustard in a mixing bowl until sugar is somewhat dissolved. Pour over the ham balls. In a covered dish, bake at 350 degrees F for 90 minutes.

Cakes

When I was growing up, we seldom had dessert, but Mom was always sure to make each child a special birthday cake complete with ornate decorations and writing.

Chocolate Trilogy Cake

Chocolate cake mix

Ganache:
3 cups 30 percent cocoa Ghirardelli baking chocolate chips
1/2 cup heavy cream

French Silk Filling:
1 cup cold butter
1/2 cup shortening
3/4 cup cocoa powder
3 cups powdered sugar
4 eggs

Bake cake mix by following the directions on the box. Divide the batter into two 9-inch round cake pans. Cool completely. Cut each cake layer in half horizontally to make a total of four layers. Wrap each layer with plastic wrap and freeze. Using an electric mixer with a whisk attachment, cream the butter and shortening together. Slowly add the cocoa and powdered sugar. Once the powders are fully incorporated with butter and shortening, turn the mixer on high for 3 to 4 minutes. While the mixer is still running on high, add the eggs one at a time until they are no longer visible. Mix for an additional 4 minutes, scraping bowl well.

Take the cake layers out of the freezer. Place 1 layer of cake on a cake stand and frost with 1 cup of the French Silk filling. Repeat with the remaining layers. Using an offset spatula, take any extra filling off the sides of the cake and make it smooth. Wrap with plastic wrap and place in the freezer for at least 1 hour.

Place baking chocolate chips in a heat-proof bowl. Heat the cream in a small saucepan over medium heat until small bubbles form along the sides. Pour the cream over the chocolate and let rest for a few minutes. Slowly stir until chocolate has melted completely. Let ganache cool slightly. Then pour over the cake, allowing chocolate to spill over the edges. Using a large offset spatula spread the ganache until smooth.

Angel Coconut Torte (Cake)

Made the 2007 *Des Moines Register*'s list of the Top
100 Things to Eat in Iowa Before You Die

White cake mix
1 (16-ounce) can cream of coconut

1/3 cup shredded coconut, sweetened

3–4 cups heavy whipping cream

1/2 cup sugar

Make cake according to directions on the box using the egg white
method. Divide the batter into two 9-inch round greased cake pans.
Bake at 350 degrees F for 24 to 26 minutes. Cool completely. Cut each
cake layer in half horizontally to make a total of 4 layers.

Place a large piece of plastic wrap on counter. Lay 1 cake layer, cut side
up, on the plastic wrap. Pour about 1/4 cup cream of coconut over the
layer and spread evenly with an offset spatula. Wrap with plastic wrap
and freeze. Repeat with all layers. Allow cake to freeze for at least 1 hour.

In a mixing bowl with a whisk attachment, whisk cream and sugar until
stiff. Take the cake layers out of the freezer. Place 1 layer down on a
cake stand with the cut side up. Frost the cake with whipped cream and
repeat with the remaining layers. Frost the top and sides of the cake with
the rest of the whipping cream. Top with shredded coconut.

Peppercorn's Carrot Cake

2 1/4 cups flour

1 1/2 cups sugar

2 teaspoons baking soda

2 teaspoonsground cinnamon

1/2 teaspoon salt

1/4 teaspoon ground allspice

1/4 teaspoon ground ginger

1/8 teaspoon ground cloves

1/8 teaspoon ground nutmeg

1 (8-ounce) can pineapple, crushed

3/4 cup mayonnaise

3/4 cup chopped pecans

1/2 cup shredded coconut, sweetened

2 cups shredded carrots

3 eggs

In a large mixing bowl, combine flour, sugar, baking soda, cinnamon, salt, allspice, ginger, cloves, and nutmeg. Making a well in the middle, add the remaining ingredients. Mix batter well. Divide the batter into two 9-inch round greased cake pans. Bake at 350 degrees F for 33 to 35 minutes. Cool completely. Frost with your favorite cream cheese frosting or the recipe listed at the end of this section.

ON TO STATE

ON TO STATE

Good Luck Martha & Mary

JAN • 66

JAN • 67

It is hard to imagine the energy it took my Mom, Joan, to raise nine children. We did not have much when we were growing up and wore hand-me-down clothing, but I always felt that we had enough. Despite our tight budget, Mom made a point to bake all nine of us a birthday cake. She always looked at ease working in the kitchen and the garden, raising chickens, and doing laundry. I loved it when I could help her with her work. I know I haven't thanked her enough for what she has done for me, but I'm thanking you now, Mom.

Joan's Rhubarb Cake

2 cups brown sugar

1/2 cup butter, softened

2 eggs

1 cup sour milk (1 tablespoon
vinegar and 1 teaspoon soda)

1 teaspoon vanilla

2 cups flour

3 cups chopped rhubarb

In a medium bowl, combine all the ingredients and beat well. Pour into a greased 9x13 baking pan. Bake at 350 degrees F for 30 minutes.

Turtle Cake

German chocolate cake mix

3/4 cup butter, softened

1 (13-ounce) bag caramels

1/2 cup evaporated milk

1 (12-ounce) bag chocolate chips

1 cup chopped pecans

Mix cake following directions on the box, but also add the butter. Pour half of the batter into a greased 9x13 cake pan. Bake at 350 degrees F for 10 minutes. Melt the caramels with evaporated milk in a saucepan over medium heat until smooth. Pour caramel mixture over baked cake layer. Sprinkle with chocolate chips. Pour the other half of cake batter over the caramel layer. Top with pecans. Bake for an additional 30 to 40 minutes.

Zach, my firstborn, is such a joy. He has always been adventurous and loved the outdoors. I knew at an early age that he was introverted, so I tried (not always successfully) to ask him only two questions when he came home from school. I admire his patience, faith, obedience, and intelligence.

After several years away from Aplington, he has come back and is the sixth generation working on the family farm. I love to walk through his yard and see all their fruit trees, vines, vegetables, chickens, ducks, and geese. Best of all, he has blessed me with two beautiful granddaughters.

Black Russian Bundt Cake

My son, Zach's, favorite dessert

Cake:
1 box yellow cake mix
1/2 cup sugar
3.2-ounce package instant chocolate pudding
1/4 cup vodka
1/4 cup Kahlua
3/4 cups water
1 cup vegetable oil
4 eggs

Glaze:
2 cups powdered sugar
2 tablespoons Kahlua
2–3 tablespoons cold coffee

In a large bowl, combine all the ingredients for the cake and mix well. Pour batter into a greased Bundt cake pan. Bake at 350 degrees F for 40 to 45 minutes. Cool cake in the pan for 10 minutes and then invert to a cake stand or wire rack. Mix powdered sugar, 2 tablespoons of Kahlua, and cold coffee to make the glaze. Use a pastry brush to evenly glaze the cake.

Variation: Buttered Cinnamon Bundt Cake
Follow the Black Russian recipe, exchanging these ingredients:

3.2-ounce butterscotch pudding for chocolate pudding
1/4 cup butterscotch schnapps for 1/4 cup Kahlua
1/4 cup cinnamon schnapps for 1/4 cup vodka

For the glaze:
2 tablespoons butterscotch schnapps for the Kahlua
2 tablespoons water for the coffee

Crème De Menthe Cake

1 box white cake mix
3 tablespoons crème de menthe syrup
1 (13-ounce) jar hot fudge sauce

Topping:
8 ounces whipped topping
3 tablespoons crème de menthe syrup

Make cake mix following the directions on the box, but also add the crème de menthe. Pour into a greased 9x13 cake pan. Bake as directed. Cool. Spread hot fudge sauce over cake. Stir together whipped topping and crème de menthe and spread over fudge layer. Refrigerate.

Frosting

3/4 cup butter

8 ounces cream cheese

1 cup shortening

2/3 cup half-and-half

2 teaspoons vanilla

1 teaspoon almond extract

2 (2-pound) bags of powdered sugar

In a large mixing bowl, combine all the ingredients except the powdered sugar. Cream until very smooth. Slowly add the powdered sugar, beating until light and fluffy.

Pies

When I began working at the Peppercorn twenty years ago, I had never rolled out a piecrust. At one point, there was nobody else to roll them out and I was forced to give it a try. The crusts turned out awful. It was only through many hours of practice and thousands of crusts that I am able to roll out a consistent and attractive crust in a matter of a couple minutes. Julia Child said it well in her book *My Life in France*, "No one is born a great cook, one learns by doing."

Pie Crust

3 cups flour

1 cup shortening

1 teaspoon salt

1/3 cups cold water

1 egg

1 tablespoon white vinegar

In a medium mixing bowl, cut the shortening into the flour. In a separate small bowl, beat egg, water, and vinegar. Add wet ingredients to the flour mixture until dry ingredients are moistened. Shape dough into ball and let rest for 10 minutes. Roll dough into desired size and carefully place in pie plate. If you want to bake the shell, place in refrigerator for 30 minutes prior to baking. Bake at 450 degrees F for 10 to 12 minutes, checking every 4 minutes for large air bubbles. Makes 3 single pie shells.

Coconut Pecan Fudge Pie

9 1/2-inch deep unbaked pie shell

6 ounces German chocolate

1/4 cup butter

3 eggs

5 tablespoons cornstarch

1 teaspoon salt

12 ounces evaporated milk

1 teaspoon vanilla

1/2 cup shredded coconut, sweetened

1/4 cup chopped pecans

In a microwave-safe bowl, microwave German chocolate for 45 seconds. Add butter and microwave for an additional 45 seconds. Set aside to cool slightly. In a large mixing bowl, combine eggs, cornstarch, and salt. Using a whisk beat the egg mixture well. Add melted chocolate to the egg mixture and beat well. Slowly incorporate evaporated milk and vanilla. Pour into pie shell and top with coconut and pecans. Bake at 350 degrees F for 30 minutes. Cover and bake for an additional 60 minutes. Chill before serving.

French Silk Pie

9 1/2-inch baked pie shell

1 cup cold butter

1/2 cup shortening

3/4 cup cocoa powder

3 cups powdered sugar

4 eggs

1/4 cup chopped pecans

Using an electric mixer with a whisk attachment, cream the butter and shortening together. Slowly add the cocoa and powdered sugar. Once the powders are fully incorporated with butter and shortening, turn the mixer on high for 3 to 4 minutes. While mixer is still running on high, add the eggs one at a time until they are no longer visible. Mix for an additional 4 minutes, scraping bowl well. Line the bottom of pie shell with pecans. Top with chocolate mixture. Chill for at least 1 hour before serving.

Peaches 'n Cream Pie

9 1/2-inch unbaked pie shell

2 pounds canned peaches

1 cup sugar

1/2 cup flour

1 cup heavy cream

1 tablespoon vanilla

cinnamon

Drain peaches and spread evenly over the bottom of the unbaked pie shell. In a small mixing bowl, combine sugar and flour. Spread evenly over peaches. Combine the heavy cream and vanilla. Pour over sugar and flour. Sprinkle pie with cinnamon. Bake at 450 degrees F for 15 minutes. Reduce temperature to 350 degrees F and bake for an additional 35 minutes. Pie will set up as it cools.

Peanut Butter Pie

8 ounces cream cheese

1 cup powdered sugar

1 cup crunchy peanut butter

1 1/2 cup heavy whipping cream

Baked 9 1/2-inch pie shell

Using an electric mixer with a whisk attachment, cream together the cream cheese and powdered sugar until smooth. Add peanut butter and mix until smooth. Scrape the bowl several times while mixing. With the mixer on low speed, slowly add the whipping cream. When it has all been added, scrape the bowl and whisk on high for 2 to 3 minutes. Pour into baked pie shell and chill for at least 2 hours before serving.

Raspberry Parfait Pie

A best-seller

9 1/2-inch baked pie shell

4 ounces cream cheese

1/3 cup powdered sugar

1 teaspoon vanilla

1 cup heavy whipping cream

1 1/4 cups water

1/4 cup sugar

3 ounces raspberry Jell-O

12 ounces frozen raspberries

Using an electric mixer with a whisk attachment, whip cream cheese until smooth. Add powdered sugar and mix well. Add vanilla and slowly add the heavy cream, scraping the bowl every few minutes. Beat until stiff. Pour into pie shell and spread smoothly. In a small saucepan, bring water to a boil. Take the pan off the burner and add sugar and Jell-O. Whisk until all is dissolved.

Place frozen raspberries in a medium bowl and pour hot sugar/Jell-O mixture over the raspberries. Gently stir together. When the Jell-O mixture is slightly set, pour over top of the cream cheese layer. Chill for at least 1 hour before serving.

Southern Lemon Pie

9 1/2-inch unbaked pie shell

2 (14-ounce) cans sweetened condensed milk

6 egg yolks

1 cup lemon juice

Using an electric mixer with a whisk attachment, combine the sweetened condensed milk and egg yolks, using low speed. Mix until the yolks are no longer visible. Slowly add the lemon juice and increase the mixer to medium speed. Beat for 4 minutes. Pour mixture into pie shell. Bake at 350 degrees F for 20 minutes. Chill before serving.

Pecan Pie

9 1/2-inch unbaked pie shell

1 cup light corn syrup

1 1/2 cups brown sugar

1/2 teaspoon salt

2 tablespoons melted butter

2 teaspoons vanilla

5 eggs

1 1/2 cups whole pecans

In a large mixing bowl, combine all ingredients except the pecans and whisk well. Place pecans in the bottom of pie shell. Pour mixture over the pecans. Cover pie and bake at 350 degrees F for 80 to 90 minutes.

Fresh Strawberry Pie

9 1/2-inch baked pie shell

2 pints fresh strawberries, sliced

1 cup sugar

1/4 cup cornstarch

1 cup water

1/4 cup light corn syrup

1/4 cup strawberry Jell-O

4 ounces cream cheese, softened

In a small saucepan, mix sugar and cornstarch together. Add the water and corn syrup. Place saucepan on burner and bring to a boil over medium-high heat. Add the strawberry Jell-O. Take off the heat and stir until the gelatin is dissolved.

Pour hot gelatin mixture into a medium bowl over the strawberries and stir until all the strawberries are coated. On the bottom of the pie shell, spread the cream cheese evenly. Pour the strawberry filling over the cream cheese. Chill before serving.

Double Crust Raspberry Pie

2 (9 1/2-inch) unbaked pie shells

12 ounces frozen or fresh raspberries

2 apples, peeled and shredded

1 cup sugar

1/2 cup flour

1/2 teaspoon salt

1/2 teaspoon cinnamon

2 tablespoons butter

cream and decorative sugar

In a medium bowl, mix raspberries, apples, sugar, flour, salt, and cinnamon together until well blended. Pour into pie shell. Cut butter into pieces and sprinkle over the pie. Cover with extra pie shell and crimp edges. With a pastry brush, cover pie shell with a small amount of cream. Sprinkle with sugar. Bake at 375 degrees F for 1 hour.

Double Crust Apple Pie

2 (9 1/2-inch) unbaked pie shells	1 cup sugar
5 Granny Smith apples, peeled and sliced	1/2 teaspoon salt
	2 tablespoons butter
1 tablespoon cinnamon	cream and decorative sugar

Place the peeled and sliced apples in a large mixing bowl. Cover apples with sugar, flour, cinnamon, and salt. Set aside for 1 hour. Pour apple mixture into pie shell. Cut butter into pieces and sprinkle over the pie. Cover with extra pie shell and crimp edges. With a pastry brush, cover pie shell with a small amount of cream. Sprinkle with sugar. Bake at 375 degrees F for 1 hour.

Candied Apple Pie Variation:
Follow recipe for Double Crust Apple Pie, omitting topping the crust with cream and sugar. Bake pie at 375 degrees F for 1 hour. In a small saucepan, combine 1/2 cup brown sugar and 1/4 cup butter over medium heat bringing it to just under a boil. Remove from heat and add 2 tablespoons heavy cream. Stir until smooth. Add 1/2 cup chopped pecans. Pour overwarm apple pie.

Coconut Cream Pie

9 1/2-inch prebaked pie shell

1 cup of sugar

1/3 cup cornstarch

1/4 teaspoon salt

1 teaspoonalmond extract

1 1/2 cups shredded coconut, sweetened

2 1/4 cups whole milk

3 eggs, separated

2 tablespoons butter

1 teaspoon vanilla

1/2 teaspoon cream of tartar

1/2 cup of sugar

In a heavy-duty saucepan, combine the sugar, cornstarch, and salt. In a microwave-safe container, warm the milk for 90 seconds. Stir the milk into the saucepan, making sure that all ingredients are mixed. Turn burner to medium heat and stir regularly until thick enough to coat the back of the spoon. Remove saucepan from heat.

In a small bowl, separate the eggs. Leave the yolks in the bowl and save the whites for later. Pour a small amount of hot filling into the bowl containing the egg yolks and stir. Add another small amount of filling and stir again. Next pour the egg mixture into the saucepan containing the hot filling. Return to the stove and cook for several minutesover medium heat. Remove from heat and add the coconut, extracts, and butter. Stir until smooth. Pour into baked piecrust.

In a bowl of a stand mixer with a whisk, beat the egg whites (preferably at room temperature) on high speed until foamy. Add cream of tartar. Turn the mixer back on and slowly add 1/2 cup of sugar, 1 tablespoon at a time, until soft peaks form. Spread the meringue over the filling, sealing to the edges of the piecrust. Sprinkle with shredded coconut. Bake at 350 degrees F for 10 to 12 minutes.

Lemon Meringue Pie

9 1/2-inch prebaked pie shell

1 1/2 cups sugar

1/3 cup cornstarch

1/4 teaspoon salt

1 cup fresh lemon juice

3 eggs, separated

water

1 teaspoon lemon extract

1 teaspoon lemon zest

2 tablespoons butter

1/2 teaspoon cream of tartar

1/2 cup sugar

In a heavy-duty saucepan, combine the sugar, cornstarch, and salt. In a 4-cup liquid measuring cup, measure the lemon juice. Add 3 egg yolks and enough water to measure 2 1/4 cups. Add this to the saucepan, making sure that all ingredients are mixed. Turn the burner onto medium heat, stirring regularly until thick enough to coat the back of the spoon. Remove from heat and add the lemon extract, lemon zest, and butter. Stir until smooth. Pour into baked piecrust.

Using a stand mixer with a whisk, beat the egg whites (preferably at room temperature) on high speed until foamy. Add cream of tartar. Turn mixer back on and slowly add 1/2 cup of sugar, 1 tablespoon at a time, until soft peaks form. Spread the meringue over the filling, sealing to the edges of the piecrust. Bake at 350 degrees F for 10 to 12 minutes.

Strawberry Rhubarb Pie

2 (9 1/2-inch) unbaked pie shells

cream and decorative sugar

3 cups strawberries, fresh

3 cups rhubarb

1 cup sugar

1/2 cup flour

1/4 teaspoon salt

1 teaspoon cinnamon

2 tablespoons butter

Clean and hull strawberries. Either slice or quarter them. Cut rhubarb into 1/2-inch pieces. In a large mixing bowl, combine the two fruits. Cover with sugar, flour, cinnamon, and salt. Set aside for 15 minutes. Pour fruit mixture into unbaked pie shell. Cut butter into pieces and sprinkle over the pie. Cover with second pie shell and crimp edges. With pastry brush, cover pie shell with a small amount of cream. Sprinkle with sugar. Bake at 375 degrees F for 1 hour.

Custard Pie

9-inch unbaked pie shell

4 slightly beaten eggs

1/2 cup sugar

1/2 teaspoon salt

1 teaspoon vanilla

1 teaspoon almond extract

2 1/4 cup scalded milk

nutmeg

In a medium mixing bowl, blend eggs, sugar, salt, vanilla, and almond extract. Whisk well so the egg yolks are no longer visible. Slowly add scalded milk (where milk has been microwaved for 90 seconds). Pour into unbaked pie shell. Bake at 400 degrees F for 30 minutes. Remove from oven and sprinkle with nutmeg. Let cool on pie rack for 15 minutes. Chill before serving.

Pumpkin Pie

9-inch unbaked pie shell

1 cup sugar

1 teaspoon cinnamon

1/2 teaspoon ginger

1/4 teaspoon nutmeg

1/8 teaspoon ground cloves

1/2 teaspoon salt

2 eggs

1 (15-ounce) can pumpkin

1 (12-ounce) can evaporated milk

In a small mixing bowl, combine sugar, spices, and salt. Add eggs and pumpkin and whisk well. Slowly add evaporated milk and whisk until smooth. Pour filling into unbaked pie shell. Bake at 425 degrees F for 15 minutes. Turn oven down to 350 degrees F. Bake for an additional 40 minutes. Remove from oven and let cool on pie rack 15 minutes before chilling.

Cheesecakes

Snickers Cheesecake

2 1/4 cups duplex sandwich cookies, crushed

1/4 cup chopped walnuts

5 tablespoons melted butter

24 ounces cream cheese

14 ounces sweetened condensed milk

3 eggs

1 tablespoon vanilla

2 tablespoons white rum

2 Snickers bars, finely chopped

Crust:
Mix cookie crumbs, walnuts, and butter together. Press mixture into the bottom of a 9-inch springform pan.

Filling:
Using a stand mixer with a whisk, beat cream cheese until smooth. Add sweetened condensed milk, scraping bowl frequently, and beat again until smooth. With the mixer on low speed, add eggs one at a time, followed by the vanilla and rum. Beat for 1 minute longer. Stir in the chopped Snickers bars by hand. Pour mixture into prepared springform pan. Tap several times on the counter to release any air pockets. Bake at 350 degrees F for 35 minutes. Remove from the oven and run a knife along the outside of the cheesecake to release it from the springform. Cool on rack. Chill before serving.

Raspberry Swirl Cheesecake

2 cups crushed vanilla sandwich cookies

1/4 cup sugar

5 tablespoons melted butter

24 ounces cream cheese

14 ounces sweetened condensed milk

3 eggs

1/4 cup lemon juice

3/4 cup raspberry topping, sauce or jam

Crust:
Mix cookie crumbs, sugar, and butter together. Press mixture into the bottom of a 9-inch springform pan.

Filling:
Using a stand mixer with a whisk, beat cream cheese until smooth. Add sweetened condensed milk, scraping bowl frequently, and beat again until smooth. With the mixer on low speed, add the eggs one at a time followed by the lemon juice. Beat for 1 minute longer. Pour mixture into prepared springform pan. Tap several times on the counter to release any air pockets. Bake at 350 degrees F for 35 minutes. Remove from the oven and run a knife along the outside of the cheesecake to release it from the springform. Cool on rack. Chill before serving.

Pumpkin Cheesecake

2 cups crushed vanilla sandwich cookies

5 tablespoons melted butter

1/4 cup brown sugar

1 teaspoon ginger

20 ounces cream cheese

14 ounces sweetened condensed milk

3 eggs

1 (15-ounce) can pumpkin

1 teaspoon cinnamon

2 tablespoons white rum

1 tablespoon vanilla

Crust:
Mix cookie crumbs, butter, brown sugar, and ginger together. Press into a 9-inch springform pan.

Filling:
Using a stand mixer with a whisk, beat cream cheese until smooth. With the mixer on low speed, add eggs one at a time followed by the vanilla and rum. Beat for 1 minute longer. Add pumpkin and cinnamon and stir by hand until well combined. Pour mixture into prepared spring form pan. Tap several times on the counter to release any air pockets. Bake at 350 degrees F for 40 minutes. Remove from the oven and run a knife along the outside of the cheesecake to release it from the springform. Cool on rack. Chill before serving.

My Dad and three brothers—Mike, Paul, and Peter—all served
in the military. I am eternally grateful for their service.